Dress Up:

Written by Alwyn Evans

Contents

Introduction   4

Chapter 1 Traditional Clothing   8

Chapter 2 Clothes for Special Occasions   14

Chapter 3 Costumes for the Theater   20

Chapter 4 Cool Creations   26

Index and Bookweb Links   32

Glossary   Inside back cover

Rigby

Chapter Snapshots

Introduction PAGE 4

People wear different clothes for different occasions.

1 Traditional Clothing

PAGE 8

Traditional clothing tells us about the cultures of the groups who wear it.

2 Clothes for Special Occasions

PAGE 14

Certain ceremonies and jobs require specific types of clothing.

3 Costumes for the Theater

PAGE 20

Plays tell stories. The theater costumes help audiences know more about the play and the characters in it.

4 Cool Creations

PAGE 26

You could be a costume designer! The role of a designer comes to life through the procedure for planning a costume.

"The way a person dresses may affect the way you see and feel about that person."

Introduction

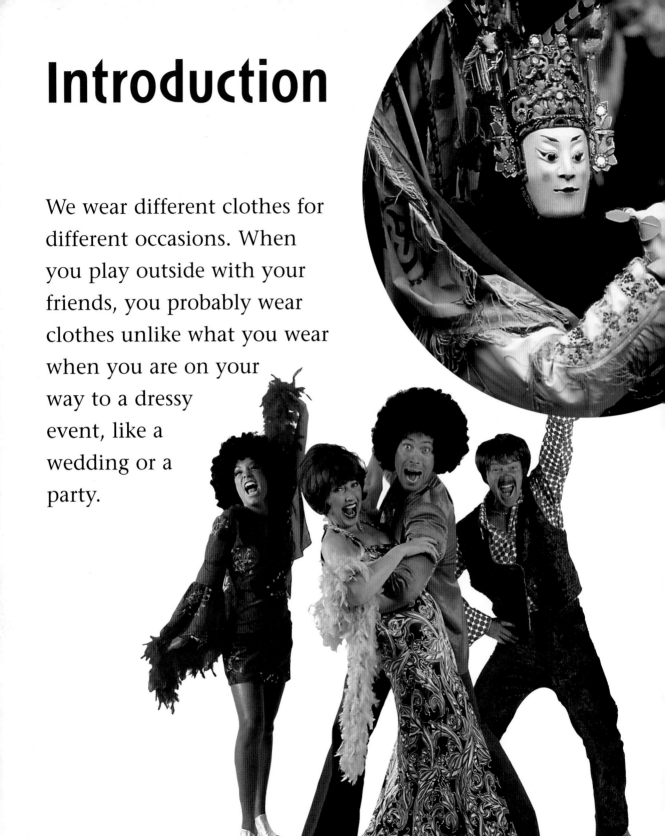

We wear different clothes for different occasions. When you play outside with your friends, you probably wear clothes unlike what you wear when you are on your way to a dressy event, like a wedding or a party.

The people on these pages have dressed up for special occasions. Can you guess what those might be?

Look at this picture.
What do you see?

What differences do you see?
Do you see the same person
beneath the costume?

Yes, it is the same person!
The way a person dresses may
affect the way you see and feel
about that person.

Since the earliest times, people have dressed in ways that show something about themselves. What are the boys in this picture showing about themselves by the way they are dressed? They are showing that they are baseball players and they belong to the same team. A baseball team's uniforms makes it easier for the spectators to tell the teams apart.

1 Traditional Clothing

Many people from different countries wear traditional clothing for celebrations and ceremonies.

People dress up for traditional dances and songs. These dances and songs teach us about these people.

Traditional Costumes Today

Today, many different groups wear traditional costumes. Sometimes, Japanese women wear kimonos to special events, like a wedding.

Mongolian people in traditional dress

The Quechua Indians of South America wear brightly colored ponchos and shawls as their everyday clothes.

Traditional costumes also include masks and jewelry. These may be made from animal teeth, claws, and feathers. These things have special meanings.

Members of the Crow nation dress in traditional clothing to celebrate the days when buffalo were plentiful. This headdress is called a *roach*. It is made of feathers and porcupine hair.

Holidays

Holidays are an important time for dressing up in traditional clothing. Many families in the United States who share a common heritage dress in the tradition of that heritage to celebrate holidays. Do you have a special way of dressing on holidays?

Members of an African American family dress in traditional African clothing to celebrate Kwanzaa.

A Cinco de Mayo celebration in California provides an opportunity for Mexican Americans to celebrate their heritage through dress.

2 Clothes for Special Occasions

Dressing up for special occasions is a way of marking the importance of the day. The clothing worn on these days often symbolizes something. For example, a bride wears a white wedding gown symbolizing purity. The color of the tassel on a college graduate's cap shows the student's field of study.

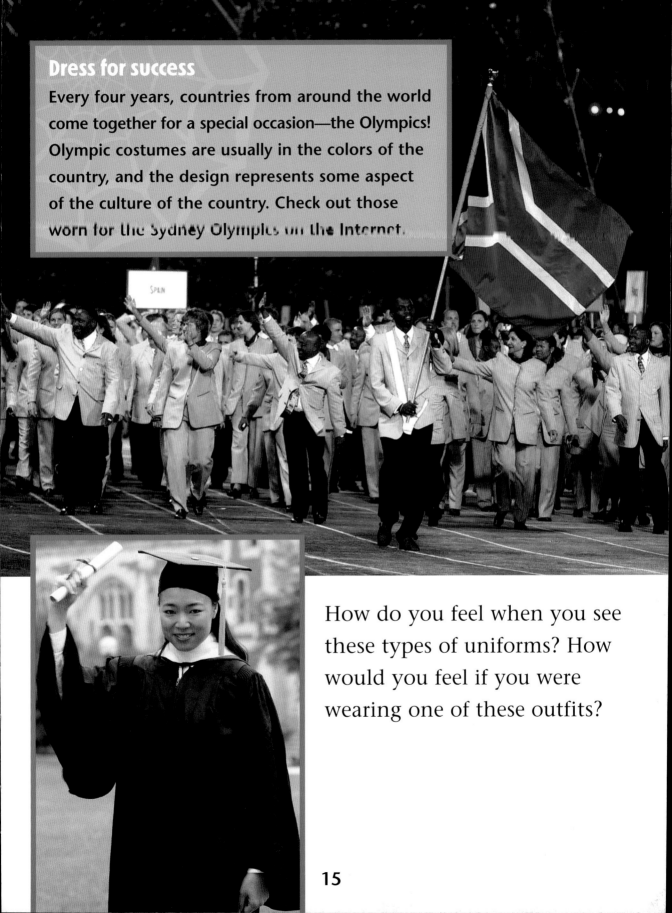

Dress for success

Every four years, countries from around the world come together for a special occasion—the Olympics! Olympic costumes are usually in the colors of the country, and the design represents some aspect of the culture of the country. Check out those worn for the Sydney Olympics on the Internet.

How do you feel when you see these types of uniforms? How would you feel if you were wearing one of these outfits?

Dressing for Work

Many people wear uniforms that help them perform their job.

Fireproof clothing protects firefighters as they battle blazes and enter flaming buildings.

What other jobs can you name that require uniforms?

A police officer's uniform is easy to recognize for those who need help.

Mail carriers spend a lot of time outdoors. Uniform shorts help them stay cool on hot summer days.

Clothing—Then and Now

Times change and clothing changes. Look at the Then and Now pictures on this page. How has the clothing worn by these people changed over the years? What might be the reasons for those changes?

Then – Diving in 1939 requires lots of gear.

Now – How can these divers breathe underwater without returning to the water's surface?

Now – Commander Eileen Collins is the first woman to command a Space Shuttle mission.

Then – Dressed in a leather flying suit, test pilot Paul King is ready to take to the skies in the year 1925.

3 Costumes for the Theater

At the theater or ballet, the audience watches and listens to live actors. The way the actors dress helps the audience recognize characters, work out when the action takes place, and tell how much time has passed in the play. Stage settings, music, and other sound and visual effects also help tell the story.

Look at these stage settings carefully. Can you tell when each of these plays takes place by what the characters are wearing? Can you tell where each play takes place?

Costumes 'Speak' to the Audience

A costume gives us information about the characters wearing it. The costumes 'tell' us if the characters are rich or poor, what job they might do, and even what country they might be from.

The costumes and sets also tell us what time the story takes place—whether it's long ago, ten years ago, or in the future.

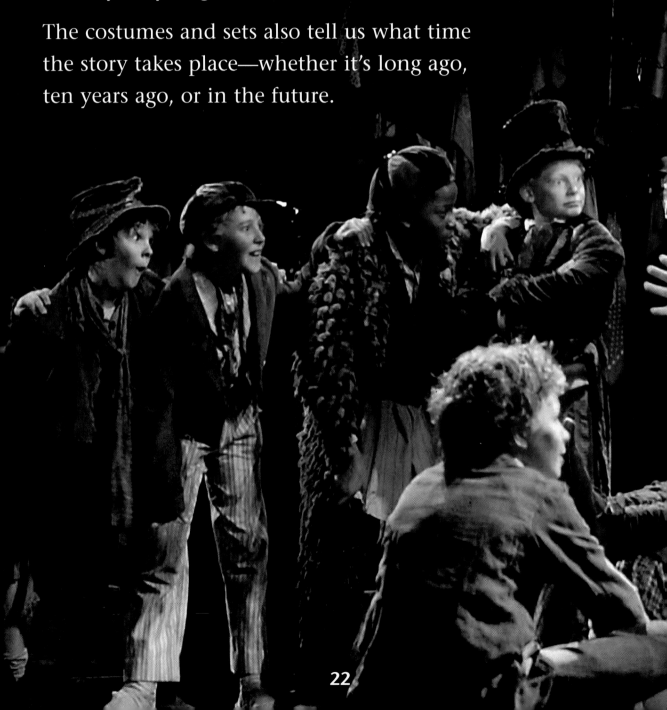

At what time in the past do you think this play is set? What clues do the costumes give you that help you guess what this popular show is called?

This ballet, called the *Nutcracker Suite*, tells a story about toys coming to life when the owners are asleep.

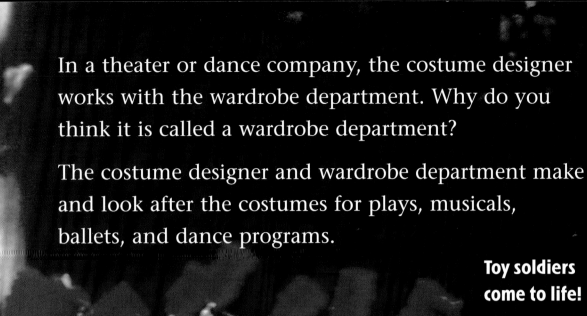

In a theater or dance company, the costume designer works with the wardrobe department. Why do you think it is called a wardrobe department?

The costume designer and wardrobe department make and look after the costumes for plays, musicals, ballets, and dance programs.

Toy soldiers come to life!

4 Cool Creations

Costumes can include:

- makeup,
- face or body paint,
- masks,
- hats, crowns, hoods, or other head wear,
- footwear,
- clothes made of carefully chosen fabrics and designed to tell something about the character, and
- a wide range of accessories.

You Be the Costume Designer

1 **Rumpelstiltskin's Characteristics:**
- a wrinkly and evil-looking man
- has a long crooked nose
- has an ugly mouth and broken teeth
- has thin white hair
- has skinny legs, arms, and body
- has long fingers with big gold rings and cracked dirty nails
- likes gold and jewels

List everything you know about your character. Are you a person, a dog, a robot, an alien? Are you male or female? How old are you? What do you look like? What job do you do? What do you like?

2 **Rumpelstiltskin Wears:**
- crumpled, floppy, blue silk pants
- a dark green velvet coat
- a tall black hat
- old black shoes with big gold buckles
- lots of jewels and carries a walking stick

List the outfits (for humans) or coverings (for animals, robots, etc) that your character would wear.

3 Draw rough sketches of the character in costume, until the design is right.

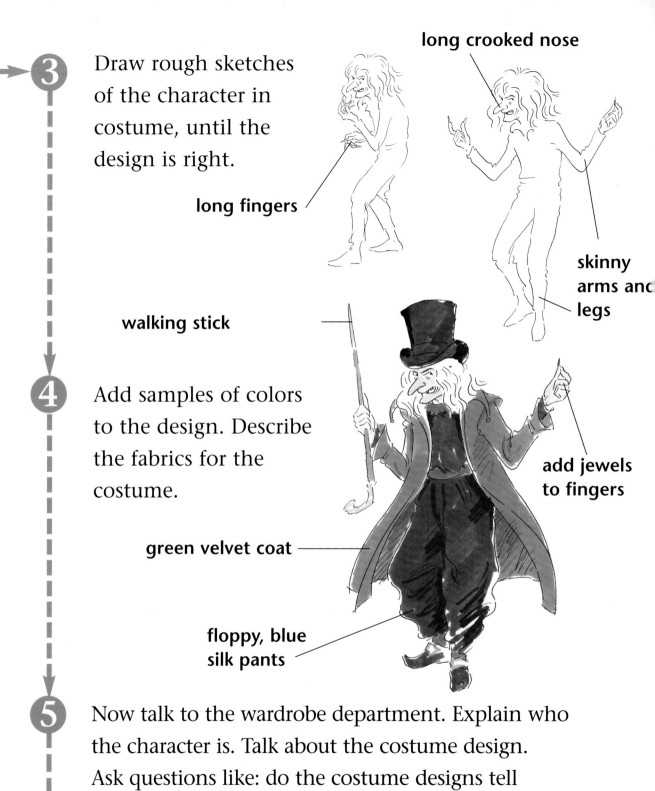

long crooked nose

long fingers

skinny arms and legs

walking stick

4 Add samples of colors to the design. Describe the fabrics for the costume.

add jewels to fingers

green velvet coat

floppy, blue silk pants

5 Now talk to the wardrobe department. Explain who the character is. Talk about the costume design. Ask questions like: do the costume designs tell you something about the character?

It's time to draw and color the final
draft of the costume design.

Teamwork

And here's the team who will make up your design.

Wardrobe designers add finishing touches to this costume.

The hats are laid out. Each character's hat is labelled.

IGOR

VALENTIN

MAXI...

EV...

Wigs backstage.

Why not try some costume designing of your own!

31

Index

baseball players 7
Cinco de Mayo 12
costume design 25, 27–31
Crow nation 11
firefighters 16
holidays 12–13
kimono 8
Kwanzaa 13
mail carriers 17
Mongolian people 8
Nutcracker Suite 24–25
police officer 16
Quechua Indians 9
theater costumes 20–31
traditional clothing 8–13
uniforms 7, 15, 16–17

Bookweb Links

Key to Bookweb Fact Boxes
- ■ **Arts**
- ■ **Health**
- ■ **Science**
- ■ **Social Studies**
- ■ **Technology**

Read more Grade 3 books in Bookweb and Bookweb Plus about dressing up, and the special clothes people wear:

Silks, Satins, or Synthetics — Nonfiction

The Butcher, the Baker... — Nonfiction

Home Safety — Nonfiction

Action Safety — Nonfiction

Making Music — Fiction